SCIENCE FRONTIERS

EXTREME STRUCTURES

MEGA-CONSTRUCTIONS OF THE 21ST CENTURY

DAVID JEFFERIS

Crabtree Publishing Company
www.crabtreebooks.com

INTRODUCTION

Wow! That is the word you will use when you see the structures in this book for the first time.

Building big is nothing new. Thousands of years ago, peoples of ancient lands were erecting giant-sized structures, some of which still stand today. The biggest ancient structure is the 4,600-year-old Great Pyramid of Giza, built as an enormous **tomb** for the Egyptian Pharaoh Khufu.

The extreme structures of the 21st century are mostly built for business or transportation purposes, such as office buildings, visitor centers, long bridges, and deep tunnels.

Crabtree Publishing Company
www.crabtreebooks.com

PMB 16A
350 Fifth Ave.
Ste. 3308
New York
NY 10118

616 Welland Ave
St. Catharines, ON
Canada
L2M 5V6

Edited by
Isabella McIntyre

Coordinating editor
Ellen Rodger

Editors
Rachel Eagen
Adrianna Morganelli

Production Coordinator
Rosie Gowsell

Technical consultant
Mat Irvine FBIS

Created and produced by
David Jefferis/BuzzBooks

©2006 David Jefferis/BuzzBooks

Cataloging-in-Publication Data
Jefferis, David.
  Extreme structures : mega-construction of the 21st century / David Jefferis.
    p. cm. -- (Science frontiers)
  Includes bibliographical references and index.
  ISBN-13: 978-0-7787-2858-0 (rlb)
  ISBN-10: 0-7787-2858-7 (rlb)
  ISBN-13: 978-0-7787-2872-6 (pbk)
  ISBN-10: 0-7787-2872-2 (pbk)
  1. Structural engineering--Juvenile literature. 2. Buildings--Juvenile literature. I. Title. II. Series.
  TA634.J34 2006
  624.1--dc22
                    2005036406
                    LC

Pictures on these pages, clockwise from above left:
1 Two huge hotels form part of a giant leisure complex in Dubai, Middle East.
2 Britain's Spinnaker Tower includes a glass-sided elevator to speed tourists to see the spectacular view from the top.
3 Office buildings in Hong Kong, China.
4, 5 Strange shapes mark the US Walt Disney Concert Hall and the Czech Dancing House building. Both were designed by architect Frank Gehry.

CONTENTS

BIGGER AND BIGGER

More giant structures are built today than ever before, which is made possible by modern building methods. Most big cities have a cluster of high-rises in central areas.

The oldest surviving extreme structures were built in ancient Egypt. The Pyramid of Djoser was erected there nearly 4,800 years ago. Many of these early structures still stand. Today, few extreme structures are built to last more than 100 or 200 years, and many structures will be replaced long before they are that old.

Until the 1900s, big buildings were usually made from stone. Today, stone is usually used only for decoration. Steel, concrete, glass, and plastic are the materials most used in construction today.

▲ New York's 22-story Flatiron Building, built in 1902, was one of the city's first skyscrapers.

▲ In some cities, tall office buildings and two or three story housing units are built in the same area.

CLASSICAL EXTREMES

Many of today's structures are based on the work of past builders. The Great Pyramid in Egypt was erected about 4,600 years ago as a tomb for Pharaoh Khufu, and is the tallest pyramid ever built. It stands 455 feet (139 meters) high.

The Parthenon in Athens, Greece, was built nearly 2,500 years ago as a temple to the goddess Athena. The Parthenon's builders thought very hard about the design.

The stone columns were specially shaped to curve upward, making the building look symmetrical or even.

St. Peter's Basilica in Rome was finished in 1626 and has a huge dome more than 138 feet (42 meters) across. Heavy domes spread their weight outward at the base. St. Peter's is slightly egg-shaped. The weight goes straight down, which made the supports and foundations easier to build.

Great Pyramid of Giza, Egypt

Parthenon, Greece

St. Peter's Basilica, Italy

▲ ▶ Pyramid, column, and dome are three of the basic architecture shapes, along with the cube.

Many Asian countries are becoming popular spots for building new structures. Populations there are growing fast, so planners are coming up with ideas for the future, such as a tower that will house 100,000 people.

◀ The CN Tower in Toronto, Canada, opened in 1976 as the world's highest observation tower. It stands 1,815 feet (553 meters) high and attracts more than two million visitors each year.

5

HIGH-TECH DOMES

The dome at Expo 67

Postage stamp

▲ One of Buckminster Fuller's domes was built for the Expo 67 fair, held in Montreal, Canada (top). In 2004, Fuller's picture was featured on a U.S. postage stamp to honor his work.

Building giant domes is possible largely because of the pioneering work of U.S. architect Buckminster Fuller, who developed lightweight geodesic domes.

Domes built on Fuller's principles have big advantages over other large structures. These domes are lightweight and do not need support columns inside. Larger domes are more stable than smaller domes. In theory, an entire city could be covered with a dome. Domes are usually made of steel or aluminum tubes, joined at the ends to make a curving surface of triangles or **hexagons**.

Hexagons use three layers of ETFE transparent foil

Trucks shifted two million tons (1.8 million tonnes) of dirt during construction

▲ Eden's biomes have no glass panels, as these are thought to be too heavy, and dangerous if they broke. Instead, hexagons of ETFE plastic are used. The largest hexagon is 36 feet (11 meters) across.

The world's biggest greenhouse was built in an old clay pit in Cornwall, England. The Eden Project environmental center has huge domes called **biomes**, which simulate tropical and Mediterranean climates. The biomes hold more than 100,000 plants, including banana, rubber, teak, and mahogany trees.

▲ Eden's humid tropical biome has waterfalls, pools, and thousands of heat-loving plants.

The dome is almost 206 feet (63 meters) high

◀ **The Expo 67 dome in Montreal is now the home of an environment center, based on a water theme. The original dome was weatherproofed by 1,900 clear panels, but they were burned in a fire.**

The dome weighs about 661 tons (600 tonnes)

COULD WE BUILD A DOMED CITY?

The idea of covering a city with a giant dome dates back to the early days of science fiction. One story imagined dome cities flying through the clouds, 10,000 years in the future.

We are a long way from seeing flying cities, but we can build big domes today. A geodesic dome is the only human-made structure where bigger means stronger. A dome usually takes little time to build.

The tube sections are lightweight. Domes can resist high winds, but it is difficult to calculate how they will react to a collision — some tubes may break, and others may not.

Buckminster Fuller hoped that his domes would be popular as homes, but a small dome wastes a lot of interior space, unless beds, shelves, and other items are specially made to fit within the curving edges.

A 1960s sketch shows part of New York under a giant dome

SKYSCRAPERS

Skyscrapers **are very tall buildings. They are usually at least 500 feet (153 meters) in height.**

The first skyscrapers were built in Chicago, Illinois, and St. Louis, Missouri, in the 1890s. Technical advances, such as super-strong steel, high-speed elevators, and powerful water pumps, made it possible to build them so high.

The skyscrapers were built quickly using steel frames, which made them very strong. Elevators made it easy for people to travel up and down many stories. Water pumps allowed running water to reach the highest floors of the skyscrapers.

▲ New York is still the leading "skyscraper city," with famous buildings such as the Empire State Building and the art deco-styled Chrysler Building (shown above by the arrow).

▼ Eight of the world's tallest skyscrapers, lined up to scale.

▲ When finished, the Burj Dubai will be the world's tallest skyscraper at more than 2,300 feet (700 meters) high.

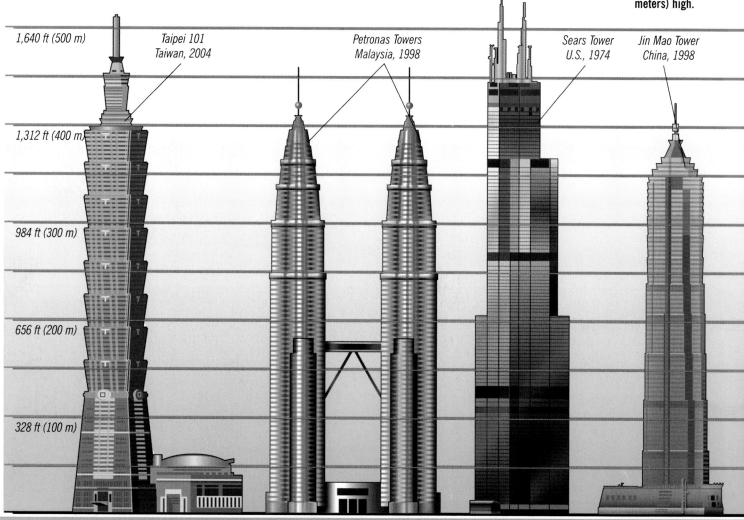

1,640 ft (500 m)

1,312 ft (400 m)

984 ft (300 m)

656 ft (200 m)

328 ft (100 m)

Taipei 101
Taiwan, 2004

Petronas Towers
Malaysia, 1998

Sears Tower
U.S., 1974

Jin Mao Tower
China, 1998

◄ In Hong Kong, the governor's residence is located next to the latest high tech office buildings.

Many countries are competing to build the tallest structures. For wealthy, powerful nations, this is a way of showing success. No skyscraper has come close to the vision of U.S. architect Frank Lloyd Wright, who sketched a concept for a mile-high (1.6 kilometer) building in 1956.

THE FIRST SKYSCRAPERS

The 1885 Home Insurance Building (HIB) in Chicago, was one of the first buildings made with a steel frame, a new technique at that time.

The steel frame dramatically cut the HIB's weight to less than half that of a traditional brick or stone building of similar size. The outer curtain walls were thin and light, because they did not have to hold the weight of the building. Local officials thought they would be too weak, and stopped construction while they checked the calculations of the architect, William Jenney, but there were no problems.

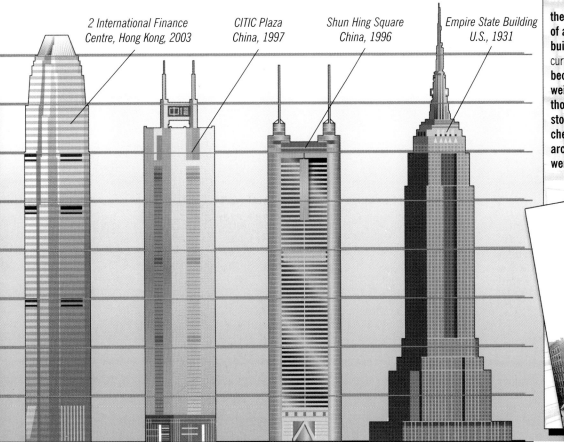

2 International Finance Centre, Hong Kong, 2003

CITIC Plaza China, 1997

Shun Hing Square China, 1996

Empire State Building U.S., 1931

COMPUTER CURVES

Using computers to design buildings makes it possible to create amazing structures with unusual shapes that swoop and soar.

A viewing deck with glass floor section

We live in an exciting age of architecture. Computers allow an architect or engineer to visualize a new design quickly and easily. If the design does not work, it can be easily revised.

◀ The Spinnaker Tower in England was built to give the city of Portsmouth a tall symbol that would attract visitors from other countries. The glass elevator and double-decker observation areas help bring trade to the area.

When is a building a work of art rather than plain architecture? That is a question that architect Frank Gehry (1929-) has tried to answer with his sculptural designs, such as his best-known building, the sculpture-like Guggenheim Museum in Bilbao, Spain. This structure is so dramatic that it has made Bilbao a popular tourist destination.

Thin metal sheets cover the outside

▲ The Guggenheim Museum, in Bilbao, Spain, is covered with shiny titanium metal panels that gleam under the sun or spotlights at night.

▲ Calatrava's Arts Museum in Valencia, Spain, opened in 2005.

The Spanish architect and engineer Santiago Calatrava (1951-) has designed many bridges, museums, and other structures. He is also a sculptor, who manages to blend his art with architecture.

Some of Calatrava's buildings could be straight from a science fiction movie, and all have elegant shapes, made possible by using **computer-aided design** systems. These systems allow Calatrava to refine the style and appearance of a new structure quickly, saving time and money.

COMPUTER-AIDED DESIGN

Computer-aided design (CAD) has been used by engineers and architects since the 1960s. Using a CAD program, any structure can be designed on screen, with its features stored in the program. Realistic visuals like the ones below are made to see whether an idea will work or needs to be changed.

CAD helps determine how the structure will stand up to high winds or earthquakes. CAD also checks the strength and thickness of the materials being used.

Once a new project is approved, CAD is used to tweak the final design, to make a list of parts needed, and other details.

ECO STRUCTURES

Extreme structures do not need to use more energy than other buildings. In fact, they are usually designed to be as energy-efficient as possible.

▲ The Torre Agbar tower in Barcelona, Spain, is cooled by a ventilation system that allows hot air to rise naturally up and out of the building.

Designing environmentally friendly, or "green" buildings is a priority for many architects. Reducing the amount of energy used to heat buildings is vital. Many new buildings use only half the power that older buildings use.

Changing the way sunlight enters a building is vital for energy conservation. Architect Norman Foster rebuilt the German Reichstag parliament building with a huge glass dome on the roof. Mirrors reflect sunlight inside to heat the building. A computerized shield tracks the sun and blocks glare.

▼ The central mirror system in the Reichstag's roof dome directs light downward. Government work is done below, giving visitors a perfect view.

A window cleaner on a "cherry picker" arm

The tower measures 590 feet (180 meters) high

◄ Triangles form the basic tower structure. They make it very strong, and lighter than a traditional office building.

This cone-shaped tower in London, England, is nicknamed "the gherkin" for its pickle shape. It is another energy-saver. Shafts in the floors let out hot air in summer, while allowing the sun's rays to heat the building in winter. The gherkin's design allows sunlight to reach deep inside, reducing the power needed for lighting.

SHOULD WE DIM THE CITY LIGHTS?

Bright neon signs lighting up the night sky could be a thing of the past if the International Dark-Sky Association (IDSA) gets its way. IDSA has two aims — to save energy, and to make the stars visible in the night skies of cities. All but the brightest stars are drowned out by light pollution in cities.

IDSA's ideas include shining lights down instead of up, turning them off when not needed, and always using energy-saving lightbulbs. Advertising signs can be turned off late at night, as can the lights in parking areas.

Can it work? Some cities in Australia and the U.S. are giving IDSA's ideas a try. The city of Rome, Italy is also interested. With 170,000 street lights, Rome could save about 40 percent on its lighting costs.

13

LUXURY LIVING

Size and comfort are features of the world's most spectacular hotels. Luxury hotels give visitors the comforts they could only dream of back home.

▲ Comfort and style are what is offered in the super-luxury hotel business.

The Luxor Hotel in Las Vegas, Nevada, is as much a theme park as a place to stay. It was designed using an ancient Egyptian theme, and includes a huge black glass pyramid and a giant **Sphinx** by the entrance.

The Luxor is enormous. It has 4,407 rooms within the 30-story pyramid and a pair of high-rises. The pyramid is 350 feet (107 meters) high, topped with the most powerful searchlight in the world.

The Burj Al Arab is a super-luxury hotel just off the beach in Dubai, United Arab Emirates. It was designed to echo the shape of a **dhow** sail boat and, at 1,053 feet (321 meters) high, it is the tallest hotel in the world. Its **atrium** is big enough to swallow New York's Statue of Liberty.

The hotel also boasts a **helipad**, but it is not at ground level. Instead, the pad is a circular dish that juts out from the hotel's roof. The 202 suites of the Burj Al Arab are all huge. Even the smallest two-bedroom suite occupies 1,830 square feet (170 square meters), or about the size of a four-bedroom house.

▶ **The Burj Al Arab has a** teflon-**coated glass fiber wall, the biggest of its kind. At night, floodlights light up the white fabric in a multi-colored display. The hotel is taller than the Eiffel Tower in Paris, France.**

◀ **The Luxor's vertical search light attracts millions of moths at night. They look like snowflakes as they flutter in the column of light.**

PYRAMID OF POWER

The Luxor was designed by Veldon Simpson. Among its features are elevators that move up the insides of the Pyramid, following the angle of the sides, rather than vertical shafts. The Luxor's enormous central atrium space is the world's biggest, with a volume of 29 million cubic feet (820,000 cubic meters).

The interior styling follows the Egyptian theme, complete with a temple-like swimming pool, and a copy of Tutankhamun's mask.

Big as the Luxor is, it is outranked by another Las Vegas hotel, also designed by Simpson. The MGM-Grand is the world's biggest hotel, with 5,005 rooms!

LEISURE ZONES

Everyone needs a vacation from time to time. Vacationers turn the leisure industry into a top money-maker, by visiting theme parks and thrill rides.

Poster advertising the Insanity ride

The 1,149-foot (350-meter) Stratosphere Tower in Las Vegas is home to the world's highest thrill rides. As extreme rides go, the "Insanity," shown here, is a winner. It has an arm that takes you over the edge of the Tower. As the seats spin faster, riders whirl upward and outward to experience being flung over the edge of the Tower, then stare straight down at the city below. Yikes!

▲ Ride designers used computer graphics to see what the "Insanity" ride would look like when finished.

◀ Other rides on the Stratosphere Tower include the Big Shot at the top (arrowed). This shoots riders straight up and down a tall mast.

Thrill rides are made to be exciting, but safe. New designs have computer-controlled safety restraints to ensure people stay in their seats. Power systems include compressed air, electric motors, and even magnets.

Theme parks owe much to Walt Disney, who opened his first park, Disneyland, in California in 1955. Today there are similar parks across the world. Cool weather countries have covered theme parks that are warm and dry.

AN INDOOR TROPICAL VACATION

For much of the year, the climate in northern Germany is cool and wet, making it an ideal place for a large, domed hall, called the Tropical Islands resort.

The 350 foot (107 meter) high hall was first built as an airship hangar, but it was reopened in 2004 as a high-tech vacation spot.

Inside, there is room for up to 7,000 people, who can stroll in a small rainforest with 500 plant species and trees growing up to 46 feet (14 meters) high. People can paddle in a lagoon fed by a waterfall and swim in the "South Seas" pools, bordered by a sandy beach.

A gas heating system keeps the hall at a steady 77°F (25°C)

◄ The Tropical Islands resort is open year-round and is especially popular during Germany's chilly winter. The sides once opened wide so that airships could glide out after construction.

The "South Seas" pools are about the same area as four Olympic-sized swimming pools

17

SUPERSPANS

People have built bridges for thousands of years. Bridges are now longer than ever, so they require high-tech construction.

▲ The Golden Gate bridge in San Francisco, California was the world's longest in 1937. The longest suspension bridge today is the Akashi-Kaikyo bridge, in Japan.

The first bridges were made of logs, and were built to cross streams. The Romans later built many bridges from stone and cement. The first iron bridge opened in 1781, across the River Severn, in England.

Today's lightest bridges are **suspension bridges**. They are held up by cables suspended from tall towers at either end. Well designed bridges can withstand high winds. Engineers have learned from their mistakes. One major design mistake was the Tacoma Narrows bridge built near Tacoma, Washington in 1940. The bridge, nicknamed galloping Gertie, swayed and dramatically collapsed in high winds.

▲ This film still shows the Tacoma Narrows collapsing in high winds.

► The Ting Kau bridge includes cables up to 1,525 feet (465 meters) in length.

▲ The Gateshead Millennium Bridge swings up so boats can pass underneath. When the walkway is reflected in the water, the bridge looks like a huge eye opening. The bridge, completed in 2001, crosses the Tyne River in England.

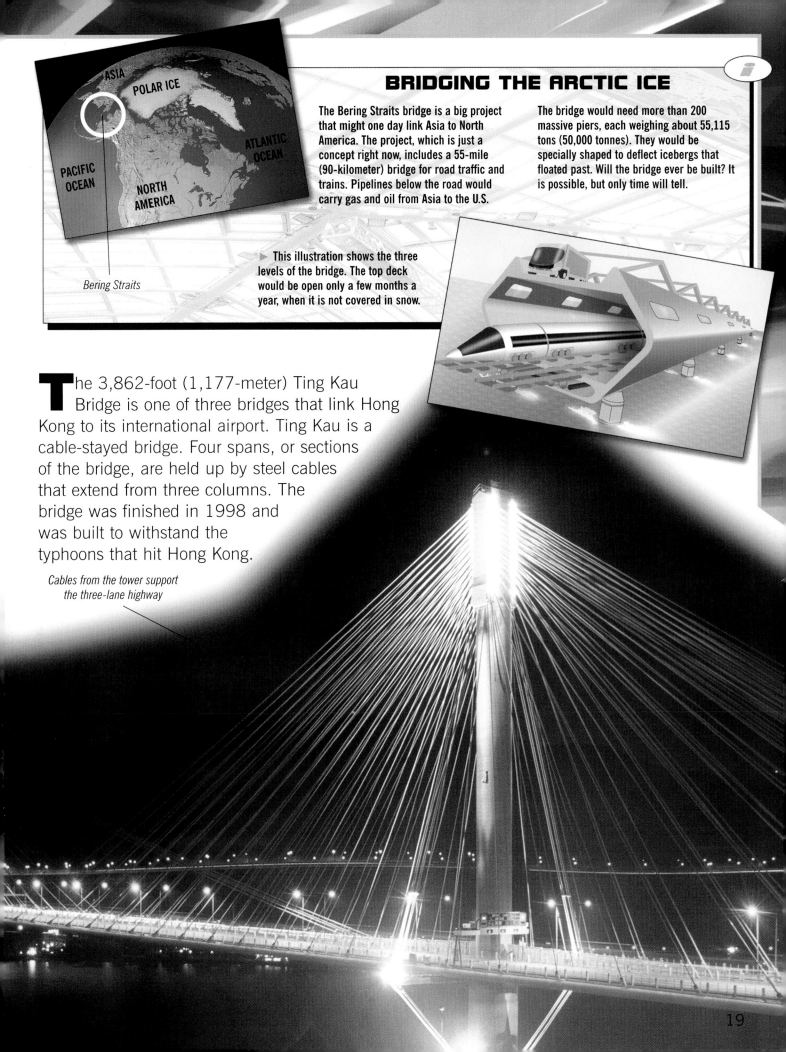

BRIDGING THE ARCTIC ICE

The Bering Straits bridge is a big project that might one day link Asia to North America. The project, which is just a concept right now, includes a 55-mile (90-kilometer) bridge for road traffic and trains. Pipelines below the road would carry gas and oil from Asia to the U.S.

The bridge would need more than 200 massive piers, each weighing about 55,115 tons (50,000 tonnes). They would be specially shaped to deflect icebergs that floated past. Will the bridge ever be built? It is possible, but only time will tell.

ASIA
POLAR ICE
ATLANTIC OCEAN
PACIFIC OCEAN
NORTH AMERICA

Bering Straits

▶ This illustration shows the three levels of the bridge. The top deck would be open only a few months a year, when it is not covered in snow.

The 3,862-foot (1,177-meter) Ting Kau Bridge is one of three bridges that link Hong Kong to its international airport. Ting Kau is a cable-stayed bridge. Four spans, or sections of the bridge, are held up by steel cables that extend from three columns. The bridge was finished in 1998 and was built to withstand the typhoons that hit Hong Kong.

Cables from the tower support the three-lane highway

DEEP DIGGERS

Massive, powerful machines allow engineers to drill tunnels under the land and seas. These new machines dig deeper and quicker than ever.

▲ This robot arm drills holes in bare rock. Explosive charges will be set in the holes for blasting.

Before a tunnel can be dug, the route has to be planned with care, especially if drilling will be done from both ends of the tunnel. Ground surveyors plan out the route that will be dug. Space satellites map the area. Computers send radio signals between Earth and space to judge the depth of the future tunnel. The latest satellite navigation systems allow a tunnel's length and height to be accurate to within 0.4 inches (one centimeter).

The world's longest underwater railway tunnel links France and England. The Channel Tunnel runs about 31 miles (50 kilometers) through solid chalk rock. It took special machines three years to bore through the rock. Today, the trip by train takes passengers only about 35 minutes.

▲ New sections of tunnel are lined with concrete to give a solid finish.

◄ The Eurotunnel has two rail lines under the sea. Trains can load and unload at both ends of the tunnel, in areas called marshalling yards. The Seikan Tunnel in Japan is a longer tunnel, but the Channel Tunnel runs for a longer stretch underwater.

▲ The face driller chews its way through the rock like a huge circular saw.

The Rail Link will consist of two tunnels, with a railroad running each way

When it opens in 2016, the Gotthard Base Tunnel will be the world's longest railway tunnel, at 35 miles (57 kilometers). The tunnel, running under the Swiss Alps and linking Switzerland to the rest of Europe, will help decrease traffic on busy mountain roads. Both passenger and freight trains will use the tunnel.

WHY BUILD A RAIL STATION INSIDE A MOUNTAIN?

The Porta Alpina station will be a stopping point midway along the Gotthard Base Tunnel. The station will allow skiers quick and easy access to the ski slopes.

Porta Alpina is being drilled out of rock, about 2,600 feet (800 meters) below the Alps. After stepping off a train, vacationers will climb aboard high-speed elevators that will lift them to their ski resorts in minutes.

Porta Alpina will connect the Gotthard Base Tunnel, running north and south, with the Rhaetian Railway/Matterhorn-Gotthard Railway, which runs east and west.

In 2016, the Porta Alpina station will be the world's deepest underground station. Convenient access to the ski slopes will draw many tourists to the Swiss Alps.

Tunnel

Porta Alpina station

Elevator shaft

MEGAPORTS

Airports and spaceports top the list of extreme structures, with giant hangars and runways built on artificial islands.

▲ The Sea Launch system is a joint venture between the U.S., Russia, Ukraine, and Norway. Here, a Zenith rocket leaves the mobile launch pad and command center, which floats in the Pacific Ocean.

Sea Launch is a floating spaceport built to launch satellites from the middle of the Pacific Ocean. Rockets can be launched from the **equator**, where the Earth's rotation speed gives rockets an energy boost.

The enormous Vehicle Assembly Building (VAB) was built in the 1960s for U.S. Apollo missions to the Moon, at Cape Canaveral, Florida. Today, the VAB is used to assemble and prepare space shuttles for flight. Rockets enter and exit through the biggest sliding doors ever made.

▼ The VAB dwarfs a space shuttle, which is being carried on the world's biggest tracked vehicle. The VAB was built to house the 360-foot (110-meter) Apollo spacecraft.

VAB doors are 456 feet or (139 meters) high

Repairs show where the VAB was damaged by a hurricane

NASA

FedEx

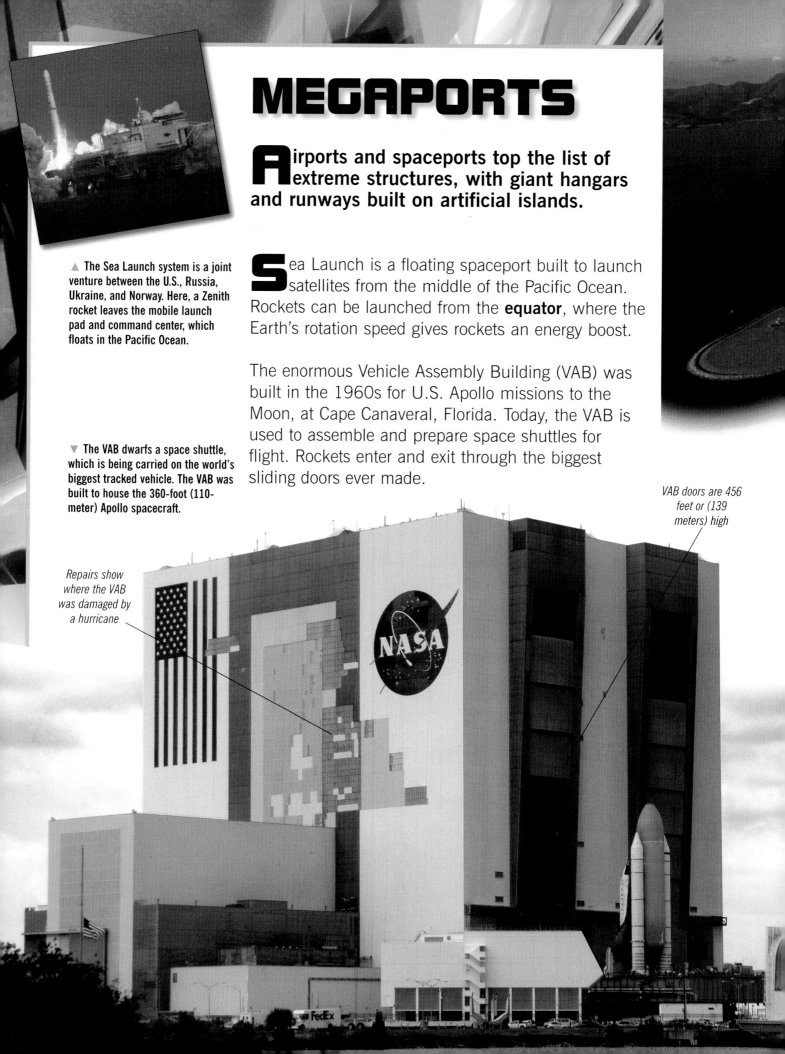

Hong Kong is a crowded island with little land to spare. When Hong Kong International airport needed to be built, airport planners realized there was no room for it on the island. The airport was made by filling the space between two smaller islands with soil. Today, 50,000 people work at the airport, and 45 million passengers use it each year. Moving sidewalks bring passengers to gates inside the terminal building, which is the world's largest, at 0.8 miles (1.27 kilometers) in length.

▲ (top) Hong Kong International being built. The small pictures show the terminal and runways.

MORE ARTIFICIAL ISLANDS

Just as impressive as Hong Kong International Airport are the islands being built from rock and sand in the Arabian Gulf. Three of the islands are shaped like giant palm trees. The Palm Jumeirah, in Dubai, is connected to the mainland by a large "trunk." It will have shops and a big tower block. The "crown" of palm fronds will have houses and apartments. The "crescent" around The Palm is seven miles (11 kilometers) long and will be home to hotels, cafés, and restaurants.

A fourth project, also in Dubai, is called The World and will consist of dozens of small islands that will make up the shape of the Earth. Water taxis will speed vacationers from island to island.

▼ The Palm Jumeirah has plenty of room for 5,000 residents and 50 hotels.

Crescent

Crown

Trunk

SCIENCE HORIZONS

The receiver is 492 feet (150 meters) above the dish

▲ Arecibo's receiver module moves back and forth on a cable system, which is suspended from three concrete towers.

Some structures, such as observatories and telescopes, are built to expand our knowledge of space and the world around us.

Built in the jungles of Puerto Rico, Arecibo is the world's biggest **radio telescope**. It measures 1,000 feet (305 meters) across. The curved "dish" of the telescope is made of 38,778 aluminum panels, held in place by steel wire mesh. Arecibo does not move like smaller telescopes do. Instead, radio signals from space bounce off it and onto an overhead receiver. Since it opened in 1963, Arecibo has been used to study distant stars, to map far-off galaxies, and to observe other planets. Arecibo has even been used as the backdrop for scenes in a James Bond movie!

The encased
sphere

The Sudbury Neutrino Observatory (SNO) in Sudbury, Ontario, Canada, is buried 6,800 feet (2,073 meters) underground. SNO is a huge sphere built to detect **neutrinos**, tiny space particles that speed through solid matter. Other particles cannot travel through the rock in which SNO is buried, so only neutrinos are detected.

▲ SNO's 39-foot (12-meter) detector sphere is filled with liquid. Neutrinos create tiny flashes in the liquid as they pass through it. The sphere is housed in a cavity the size of a 10-story building.

SENDING A MESSAGE TO THE STARS

In 1974, the Arecibo telescope beamed a message to the distant star cluster M13. The message will take 25,000 years to reach the cluster. The message was sent in a computer code which, if arranged correctly, forms a diagram with details about Earth and humans. It was hoped that aliens will receive it to learn of the human race.

The simple diagram includes the Sun and planets (yellow), a human (red), and the telescope (purple). The message was devised by a science team that included American astronomers Frank Drake and Carl Sagan.

▶ The message looks like this when decoded. Color has been added to show the different parts.

COMING SOON?

Lightweight materials and computer-aided design systems could make an architect's wildest dreams come true in the near future.

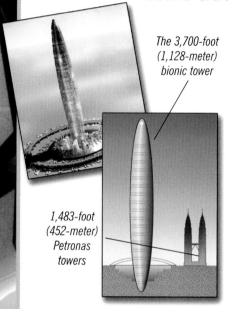

The 3,700-foot (1,128-meter) bionic tower

1,483-foot (452-meter) Petronas towers

Shanghai, China, is a fast-growing city where city planners are trying to make room for the increasing population. The **bionic** tower, a self-contained city in the sky, is designed to house about 100,000 people. Like a tree, the bionic tower would have a "root system" below ground to anchor it firmly. It would also be surrounded by a lake, which would absorb vibrations caused by frequent earthquakes, and prevent the tower from toppling.

◄ As planned, the bionic tower would have 300 stories, and take 15 years to build.

Total bridge length 12,028 feet (3,666 meters)

It has a 198 foot (60 meter) wide deck

The Strait of Messina separates Italy and the island of Sicily, in the Mediterranean Sea. By 2012, the Strait will have the world's biggest suspension bridge, with a spectacular central span of 10,827 feet (3,300 meters).

There will be six traffic lanes, two rail tracks, and two pedestrian paths for people who wish to walk or cycle across. The towers at each end will soar 1,255 feet (383 meters) above the water.

▲ The four main cables of the bridge will be spun from 44,352 separate wires.

▲ A spacecraft comes in over a Moon city. Living units, trees, shrubs, and a lake are inside. The rim wall is covered with solar panels that provide electricity from sunlight.

Scientists hope to someday build a city in one of the Moon's craters. In the illustration shown above, an air-filled plastic dome would allow people inside to live and breathe without having to wear spacesuits. A huge mirror reflects the sun's rays into the dome for heat and light.

COULD WE BUILD IN CARBON?

Carbon fiber is the lightweight and super-strong material that is widely used for the bodywork of racing cars.

It is not possible to see carbon fiber in the average building. American architects Peter Tesla and Devyn Weiser have ideas for future buildings that are lighter and stronger than anything built today by using carbon.

A carbon high-rise could be 40 stories high, with an outer shell that sweeps upward, wrapping the inside floors in a protective coating.

In the future, the way buildings are constructed could change too. Self-guided robots may replace construction workers and weave the carbon fiber shell in a spiral from the ground up.

► This is a model built to show how a carbon building tower could look.

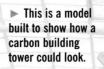

EXTREME STRUCTURES TIMELINE

Use this timeline to track the progress of extreme structures since the early days of civilization.

▲ Stonehenge is a famous early structure. The 55-ton (50-tonne) stones were brought from quarries using river rafts and tree trunk rollers. Holes were dug to position them, then they were levered into place.

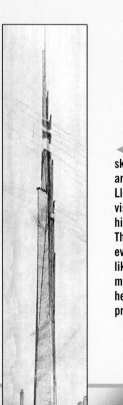

◄ This color sketch shows architect Frank Lloyd Wright's vision of a mile-high skyscraper. The highest tower ever planned is likely to be little more than half the height of Wright's proposed tower.

2778 B.C. The first pyramid is built in ancient Egypt as a stone tomb for Pharaoh Djoser.

2580 B.C. The Great Pyramid in Egypt is completed as a tomb for Pharaoh Khufu. It is the tallest pyramid ever built.

2500 B.C. Stonehenge is built in England by people hauling big stones from distant quarries. Stonehenge may have been a temple or an observatory but no one knows for certain.

447-432 B.C. The Parthenon temple is built in Athens, Greece. It is the most important surviving temple built by the ancient Greeks.

1626 The Basilica of St. Peter is finished in Rome, Italy. It has a dome designed by the artist Michelangelo that is almost as big as the Parthenon.

1779 The world's first metal bridge is built over the Severn River, England. It spans 102 feet (31 meters).

1885 The Home Insurance Building in Chicago, Illinois, is an early steel-frame building. Steel is still used for most skyscrapers.

1887-1889 The Eiffel Tower is built in Paris, France. It remains a symbol of France today.

1902 One of New York's earliest skyscrapers, the Flatiron Building, is completed. It still stands in the Manhattan District.

1931 The 102-story Empire State Building opens in New York. At 1,250 feet (381 meters), it remained the world's tallest building until 1970.

1937 The Golden Gate Bridge is finished in San Francisco. At 4,200 feet (1,280 meters), it is the world's longest bridge for 27 years.

1940 The Tacoma Narrows Bridge, Washington, collapses after it twists and buckles in high winds.

1954 Buckminster Fuller (1875-1903) is given a patent for his geodesic domes, which use triangles to make light, strong structures.

1955 Disneyland opens to visitors in California. It is the world's first big theme park, and has since been used as a pattern for many others around the world.

1956 U.S. architect Frank Lloyd Wright (1867-1959) outlines a plan for a mile-high skyscraper.

1960s Early computer-aided design (CAD) systems are developed. They are very expensive at first, but come into general use in the 1980s.

1963 Assembly work on the Vehicle Assembly Building (VAB) in Florida begins. The VAB is 525 feet (160 meters) high.

1963 The Arecibo radio telescope opens for space research in Puerto Rico. Its receiving dish is built into a natural hollow in the jungle.

1976 The CN Tower opens in Toronto, Ontario, Canada. It is the world's tallest observation tower, at 1,815 feet (553 meters) high.

1994 The Burj Al Arab hotel is opened in Dubai. It is the world's tallest hotel, at 1,053 feet (321 meters) high.

1994 The Eurotunnel underwater rail link is opened between England and France. Much of the tunnel lies 130 feet (40 meters) under the sea floor of the English Channel.

1997 The Guggenheim Museum opens in Bilbao, Spain. Designed by architect Frank Gehry (1929-), the museum is a hit with the public. Gehry's other designs follow a similar sculptural design.

1998 The world's longest bridge is opened in Japan. The Akashi-Kaikyo suspension bridge spans 6,532 feet (1,991 meters). The Ting Kau cable-stay bridge also opens in Hong Kong.

1998 Hong Kong International Airport opens with a world-leading passenger terminal.

1998 The Petronas Towers are finished in Kuala Lumpur, Malaysia. The twin tower structure becomes the world's tallest office building.

1999 Germany's Reichstag building is redesigned by British architect Norman Foster (1935-).

2000 The Eden Project opens in Cornwall, England. Its climate-controlled biomes form the world's biggest greenhouses.

2001 The Gateshead Millennium "eyelash" bridge opens in England.

2004 Tropical Islands resort opens in Germany inside the world's largest hall, the Aerium. It was built to house a huge airship that was never completed.

2012 The planned opening date for the Strait of Messina Bridge, built to cross the waters between the Italian mainland and the island of Sicily.

2016 Planned opening date for the New Gotthard Rail Link under the Swiss Alps.

▲ The Eiffel Tower is made of more than 18,000 iron sections, and was built by a construction workforce of 300 people. Maurice Koechlin (1856-1946) was the structural engineer, working for Gustave Eiffel (1832-1923), for whom the tower is named.

▲ The Shanghai World Financial Center will be almost 1,615 feet (492 meters) high. The hole in the top helps to reduce side forces from high winds. It also houses an observation gallery.

GLOSSARY

► Many large hotels often feature an atrium that forms the lobby area, giving visitors an airy and impressive view.

An explanation of some technical words and concepts used in this book.

Art deco A style of art from the 1920s and 1930s that used geometric shapes and strong colors.

Atrium A central hall or courtyard in a building that has rooms and galleries leading off it. An atrium is usually large and airy, and sometimes has a glass roof.

Basilica Originally used in ancient Rome for a court or public meeting place. The name is also used for a big church, such as St. Peter's in Rome.

Biome A group of plants and animals that live in the same habitat, such as a forest. Also used for the huge ETFE greenhouses of the Eden Project, in England.

Bionic Type of structure inspired by nature. For example, a bionic tower may have a "root system" below ground to anchor it firmly, to take in water, and to power equipment.

Computer-aided design A system that allows ideas to be fed into a computer and refined there. CAD is widely used in architecture because it speeds up design and allows changes to be made easily.

Carbon fiber A strong and lightweight material that is usually made from plastic, with small hairs of carbon mixed in, for strength. Glass fiber is another strong material that mixes plastic with fine slivers of glass.

Curtain wall Type of construction where the outer wall does not hold the building up, unlike the brick walls of a house. Instead, the wall hangs off a central steel frame, like a curtain. The building's strength is in the frame, not the walls.

Dhow A sailing boat with one or two masts.

Equator An imaginary line around the Earth dividing the north and south hemispheres. The Sealaunch rocket system fires satellites into space from here because of a boost given off by Earth's rotation. This means a rocket uses less fuel or can carry more cargo than if it was launched from closer to the poles.

ETFE A plastic material used to cover some buildings, such as the Eden Project and Allianz Stadium. It is strong, lightweight, and resists scratching. The name is short for "ethylenetetrafluoroethylene."

Geodesic dome A structure based on a network of tubes that join to form triangles. The word "geodesic" refers to the lines across the sphere made by the triangles. It is the only structure that gets stronger with size.

Helipad A landing and takeoff area for helicopters

Hexagon Any figure with six straight sides.

Neutrino A tiny particle that is created by reactions in the Sun and other stars.

Radio telescope An observatory. Stars give off radio signals as well as light waves. A radio telescope can provide extra information about objects in space.

Skyscraper A building that is at least 500 feet (153 meters) tall. The word was first used in New York, where people were amazed at the height of new buildings going up in their city during the 1890s. Many skyscrapers are built with a steel skeleton, from which glass "curtain" outer walls hang. Others are built with concrete and are reinforced with steel rods.

Sphinx The ancient Egyptian stone statue in front of the Great Pyramid. It has the body of a lion and the head of a human. The word is Greek, and means "strangler."

Suspension bridge A type of bridge where the transportation deck hangs from a series of cables. These are attached to a pair of thick cables, slung between tall towers at each end of the bridge. The suspension bridge is a popular design with engineers for two main reasons. It is much lighter than traditional bridges made of stone or brick, and it can easily span very wide rivers and valleys.

Teflon A type of nylon material used in construction as a tough and very lightweight covering. In the home, teflon is often used to coat non-stick saucepans. The name is short for "polytetrafluoroethylene."

Titanium A hard, silver-gray metal sometimes used for covering structures, such as the Guggenheim Museum in Bilbao, Spain. Aluminum, the most common metal in the Earth's crust, can also be used. Both metals resist corrosion, and do not rust after being exposed to rain.

Tomb A burial monument to the dead, such as the pyramids of ancient Egypt, which were built to honor their pharaohs, or kings.

▲ The biggest ETFE membrane in the world covers the Allianz Stadium in Germany. Lights inside the ETFE foil panels change color every few minutes, from red to white to blue.

GOING FURTHER

The Internet is a good way to keep up with the latest extreme structure projects. Here are some sites to start you off.

http://www.skyscrapercity.info
This site gives updated details of the world's latest tall buildings.

http://www.waltopia.com
This site is full of information on the legendary Walt Disney and his theme parks.

http://www.edenproject.com
A great site about the environment, especially relating to the Eden Project and its biomes.

http://science.howstuffworks.com
A fascinating site that explains how things work.

http://www.gizmag.co.uk
A site that gives the latest information on science subjects.

http://www.greatbuildings.com
A resource for looking up historical and current buildings and designers.

For more extreme structures information, use your school or local library. Design museums and visitor centers are also great places to stop by to learn more.

INDEX

Acknowledgements

We wish to thank all those individuals and organizations that have helped to create this publication. Information and images were supplied by:

Allianz Stadium, Morton Beebe, Tibor Bognar, Tony Bostrom, Corbis Photo Library, Andrey Grishin/Fotolia, R. Hackenberg, David Jefferis, Heino Kalis, Rob Matheson, Gavin Page, Gezim Radoniqi, Graphisoft, Reuters, Science Photo Library, Michael S. Yamashita, Zefa

1 2 3 4 5 6 7 8 9 0 **Printed in the U.S.A.** 5 4 3 2 1 0 9 8 7 6